Short Stories for Students, Volume 2

STAFF

Kathleen Wilson, *Editor*

Tim Akers, Pamela S. Dear, David M. Galens, Jeffrey W. Hunter, Dan Jones, John D. Jorgenson, Marie Lazzari,
Jerry Moore, Deborah A. Stanley, Diane Telgen, Polly Vedder, Thomas Wiloch, *Contributing Editors*

Jeff Chapman, *Programmer/Analyst*

Greg Barnhisel, Stephan Dziemianowicz, Tim Engles, Mary Beth Folia, Christopher Giroux, Cynthia Hallett, Karen
Holleran, Jennifer Hicks, Logan Hill, Heidi Johnson, Tamara Kendig, David Kippen, Maryanne Kocis, Rena Korb,
Kim Long, Harvey Lynch, Thomas March, Carl Mowery, Robert Peltier, Elisabeth Piedmont-Marton, Trudy Ring,

Judy Sobeloff, Michael Sonkowsky, Anne Trubek, Julianne White, Janet Witalec, *Contributing Writers*

Susan Trosky, *Permissions Manager*
Kim Smilay, *Permissions Specialist*
Sarah Chesney, *Permissions Associate*
Steve Cusack, Kelly A. Quin, *Permissions Assistants*

Victoria Cariappa, *Research Team Leader*
Michele LaMeau, Barbara McNeil, Maureen Richards, *Research Specialists*
Laura C. Bissey, Julia C. Daniel, Tamara C. Nott, Tracie Richardson,
Norma Sawaya, Cheryl L. Warnock, *Research Associates*

Mary Beth Trimper, *Production Director*
Shanna Heilveil, *Production Assistant*

Cynthia Baldwin, *Production Design Manager*
Pamela A. E. Galbreath, *Senior Art Director*

Barbara J. Yarrow, *Graphic Services Manager*
Pamela Reed, *Photography Coordinator*
Randy Bassett, *Image Database Supervisor*

Since this page cannot legibly accommodate all copyright notices, the acknowledgments constitute an extension of the copyright notice.

While every effort has been made to ensure the reliability of the information presented in this publication, Gale Research neither guarantees the accuracy of the data contained herein nor assumes any responsibility for errors, omissions or discrepancies. Gale accepts no payment for listing, and inclusion in the publication of any organization, agency, institution, publication, service, or individual does not imply endorsement of the editors or publisher. Errors brought to the attention of the publisher and verified to the satisfaction of the publisher will be corrected in future editions.

This publication is a creative work fully protected by all applicable copyright laws, as well as by misappropriation, trade secret, unfair competition, and other applicable laws. The authors and editors of this work have added value to the underlying factual material herein through one or more of the following: unique and original selection, coordination, expressions, arrangement, and classification of the information.

All rights to this publication will be vigorously defended.

Copyright © 1997
Gale Research
835 Penobscot Building
Detroit, MI 48226-4094

All rights reserved including the right of reproduction in whole or in part in any form.

This book is printed on acid-free paper that meets the minimum requirements of American National Standard for Information Sciences-Permanence Paper for Printed Library Materials, ANSI Z39.48-1984.

ISBN 0-7876-1691-5
ISSN 1092-7735

Printed in the United States of America.
10 9 8 7 6 5 4 3 2 1

The Fall of the House of Usher

Edgar Allan Poe 1839

Introduction

"The Fall of the House of Usher," written by Edgar Allan Poe in 1839, is regarded as an early and supreme example of the Gothic horror story, though Poe ascribed the term "arabesque" to this and other similar works, a term that he felt best described its flowery, ornate prose. Featuring supernatural theatrics, which critics have interpreted a number of ways, the story exhibits Poe's concept of "art for art's sake," the idea that a story should be devoid of social, political, or moral teaching. In place of a moral, Poe creates a mood—terror, in this case—through his use of language. This philosophy of "art for art's sake" later evolved into the literary movement of Aestheticism which eschewed the symbolic and preachy literature of the day—especially in England—in an attempt to overcome strict Victorian conventions. Because of his emphasis on style and language, Poe proclaimed his writing a reaction to typical literature of the day, which he called "the heresy of the Didactic" for its tendency to preach. Condemned by some critics for its tendencies toward Romanticism, a literary movement marked by melodramatic and maudlin exaggerations, "The Fall of the House of Usher" was nevertheless typical of Poe's short stories in that it presents a narrator thrust into a psychologically intense situation in which otherworldly forces conspire to drive at least one of the characters insane.

Author Biography

Poe was born January 19, 1809, in Boston, Massachusetts. His father and mother were professional actors who at the time of his birth were members of a repertory theater company in Boston. Before he was three years old both of his parents had died, and he was raised in the home of John Allan, a prosperous exporter from Richmond, Virginia. In 1915 Allan took his wife and foster son, whom he never formally adopted, to visit Scotland and England, where they lived for the next five years. While in England, Poe spent two years at the school he later described in the story "William Wilson."

Returning with his foster parents to Richmond in 1820, Poe attended the best schools available, wrote his first poetry, and, when he was sixteen years old, became involved in a romance which ended when Allan sent him to the University of Virginia at Charlottesville. There Poe distinguished himself academically, but as a result of bad debts and inadequate financial support from Allan he was forced to leave after less than a year. An established discord with his foster father deepened on Poe's return to Richmond in 1827, and soon afterward Poe left for Boston, where he enlisted in the army for lack of other means of supporting himself and where he also published his first poetry collection, *Tamerlane and Other Poems,* which the cover stated was "By a Bostonian." The book went unnoticed by readers and reviewers, and a second collection received only slightly more attention when it appeared in 1829.

That same year Poe was honorably discharged from the army, having attained the rank of regimental sergeant-major, and, after further conflict with Allan, he entered the West Point military academy. However, because Allan would neither provide his foster son with sufficient funds to maintain himself as a cadet nor give the consent necessary to resign from the academy, Poe gained a dismissal by ignoring his duties and violating regulations. He subsequently went to New York City, where his book *Poems* was published in 1831, and then to Baltimore, where he lived at the home of his aunt, Mrs. Clemm.

Over the next few years, Poe's first stories appeared in the Philadelphia *Saturday Courier,* and his "MS. Found in a Bottle" won a cash prize for best story in the Baltimore *Saturday Visitor*. Nevertheless, Poe was still not earning enough to live independently, nor did Allan's death in 1834 provide him with a legacy. The following year, however, his financial problems were temporarily alleviated when he went back to Richmond to become editor of the *Southern Literary Messenger,* bringing with him his aunt and his cousin Virginia, whom he married in 1836. The *Southern Literary Messenger* was the first of several magazines Poe would direct over the next ten years and through which he rose to prominence as one of the leading men of letters in America. Poe made himself known not only as a superlative author of fiction and poetry but also as a literary critic whose level of imagination and insight had been unapproached in American literature until that time.

While Poe's writings gained attention in the late 1830s and 1840s, the profits from his work remained meager. He was forced to move several times in order to secure employment that he hoped would improve his situation, editing *Burton's Gentleman's Magazine* and *Graham's Magazine* in Philadelphia and the *Broadway Journal* in New York. In addition, the royalties for *The Narrative of Arthur Gordon Pym, Tales of the Grotesque and Arabesque,* and other titles were always nominal or nonexistent. After his wife's death from tuberculosis in 1847, Poe became involved in a number of romances, including the one that had been interrupted in his youth with Elmira Royster, now the widowed Mrs. Shelton. It was during the time they were preparing for their marriage that Poe, for reasons unknown, arrived in Baltimore in late September of 1849. On October 3, he was discovered in a state of semiconsciousness. He died on October 7 without regaining the necessary lucidity to explain what had happened during the last days of his life.

Plot Summary

The story begins with an unnamed narrator approaching a large and dreary-looking estate. As he approaches on horseback, he muses on the images before him, the darkness of the house, the oppressiveness of the clouds above, the eye-like windows, the ragged fissure in the side of the house, the fungi on the walls, and the reflection of it all in a nearby lake. He notes that some parts of the house are crumbling and other parts are not.

He sits astride his horse, thinking about the letter he received that initiated his trip and feeling uneasy about the upcoming visit. He remembers happier times he has had with his friend, Roderick, but now, in the face of the present gloomy surroundings, these seem a distant past. Looking at the house, he makes the connection between the family mansion and the family line, both called The House of Usher (a pun on the word "house" having two different meanings). Roderick and his twin sister, Madeline, are the last members of the family line.

The narrator feels as though he is dreaming, as though these visions were "the after-dream of a reveller upon opium." This foreshadows Roderick's behavior later, when the two men meet. He is puzzled by questions about the impending visit that have no answer. "What was it—I paused to think—what was it that so unnerved me in the contemplation of the House of Usher? It was a mystery all insoluable."

He enters the house and a valet shows him to Roderick's reading room. Roderick is lying on a sofa, but arises to greet him. He looks pale and cadaverous. They exchange greetings, but Roderick's voice is unsteady and feeble. His demeanor seems more that of one suffering from drunkenness or from the use of opium. Roderick wants his friend to comfort him and share his last days with him. He says he has "suffered much from a morbid acute-ness of the senses." Only the most gentle stimulus could be endured, no hard food, loud music, strong odors, or bright lights. Only "peculiar sounds, and those from stringed instruments, which did not inspire him with horror" are tolerable. Roderick says he will perish from "this deplorable folly."

During this conversation Madeline is seen as she passes through a nearby corridor. She takes no notice of them. Roderick explains that she suffers from a malady even more baffling than his own. The physicians have said she would the of "a gradual wasting away of the person, and frequent although transient affectation of a partially cataleptical character."

After this sighting, her name is not mentioned and she is not seen alive again. The men talk together and engage in artistic endeavors, painting and writing poetry. Roderick composes some ballads, some of which he sings as he accompanies himself on the guitar. One titled "The Haunted

Palace," which Poe published apart from this story, offers a poetic rendition of the life and times of the House of Usher, including a foreshadowing of Roderick's own death. They pass some additional time together reading fantastic novels and discussing topics of a wild and horrifying nature. One such topic is Roderick's notion that the stones in his house are alive.

After a week, Roderick announces that Madeline is dead and that he needs assistance in burying her. The narrator agrees to help and they take her body, in a coffin, into a tomb that lies beneath the room in which the narrator has been sleeping. They view Madeline's body, noting the slight smile on her face and the blush on her cheeks, "Usual in all maladies of a strictly cataleptical character." They screw the lid tightly onto the coffin and close and seal a large iron door to the tomb.

During the next several days, Roderick's demeanor changes. He becomes more restless and his visage becomes more pallid. His voice grows more tremulous [shaking] and he seems to be hiding some deep secret by his peculiar speech.

About the eighth day, the narrator experiences an intense fear and dread. He rationalizes it away by believing that it is just a consequence of staying in drab and dreary surroundings. He cannot sleep, so he dresses and paces about in his apartment. He notices a light under the door and soon Roderick knocks on the door. He enters looking "cadaverously [corpse] wan" and possessed of "an evidently restrained hysteria in his whole demeanor."

Roderick opens a window to a storm, letting the wind blow violently into the room.

In an attempt to calm Roderick, the narrator takes up a copy of *Mad Trist* and begins to read. At this point, the narrator hears noises coming from below, in the tomb, but he continues to read. Each of the passages from the novel foreshadows the events of that evening. As the noises get louder, Roderick says, "we have put her living in the tomb." He springs to his feet and shrieks, "Madman! I tell you that she now stands without the door!"

The passageway in the room comes open from a strong gust of wind, and Madeline appears, bloodied and trembling. She lunges forward onto her brother, and they both fall to the floor, dead.

At this, the narrator flees quickly. As he passes over the bridge leading from the house there is a flash, the fissure in the face of the house widens, and the house crumbles "and the deep dank tarn at my feet closed sullenly over the fragments of the House of Usher."

Characters

Narrator

The unnamed narrator of the story is described as a childhood friend of Roderick Usher's. However, the narrator notes that he does not know Roderick very well because Roderick's "reserve had always been excessive and habitual." The narrator visits the Usher family house after Roderick sends him an emotional letter begging him to come. While he seems skeptical of the supernatural and tries to find rational explanations for the disconcerting things happening around him, the narrator finds himself growing increasingly disturbed by the house and the Ushers. At the end of the story, when both Roderick and Madeline die, he flees and watches the house crumble and fall into a small lake. The narrator has been described as an objective witness to the events in the story, with some suggesting he represents rationality. Others, however, have concluded that he is unreliable and that he may, in fact, have helped Roderick Usher murder his sister, or that the ending of the story is merely his hallucination.

Madeline Usher

Madeline is the twin sister of Roderick Usher and, along with her brother, is one of the only two surviving members of the Usher family. She is terminally ill and suffers fits of catalepsy, meaning she appears rigid and does not move for long periods of time. The narrator of the story, who sees her only briefly before she dies, regards her with "an utter astonishment not unmingled with dread." When Madeline dies, her brother and the narrator temporarily bury her in a vault on the first floor with "a faint blush upon the bosom and the face" and a "suspiciously lingering smile upon the lip." At the end of the story, she mysteriously emerges from her tomb, only to the with her brother. Madeline's fleeting appearance in the story serves to heighten the horror and suspense of the situation. Some critics have suggested that Madeline's illness is the result of a long history of incestual breeding in the Usher family; others believe that she possesses evil powers and is, in fact, a vampire.

Roderick Usher

Roderick Usher is the last surviving male of the Usher family. Like many of his ancestors, he has an artistic temperament, engaging in such activities as writing and playing music and painting. Described as extremely pale, with weblike hair and dark eyes, he is also a hypochondriac and is unable to tolerate such physical stimulation as bright light, the scent of flowers, and peculiar sounds. Believing that the Usher family estate is evil and that the Usher family is cursed, Roderick lives in a state of constant fear and agitation. When his twin sister Madeline dies, Roderick falls into even deeper despair and, according to the narrator, seems to be "laboring with some oppressive secret." At the end of the story, Madeline emerges from her tomb, and they both die. Roderick's anguished mental state and odd behavior have been interpreted in numerous ways. Some have speculated that he is agonizing over the Usher family secret of incest while others have suggested that Roderick represents the troubled artistic temperament. Finally, those who read "The Fall of the House of Usher" as purely a supernatural horror story state that Roderick represents evil.

Themes

"The Fall of the House of Usher," told from the point of view of an unnamed narrator, is the story of twin siblings Roderick and Madeline Usher, the last surviving members of the Usher family.

Evil

"The Fall of the House of Usher" addresses the nature and causes of evil. Poe creates an atmosphere of evil in the story through the unnamed narrator's descriptions of the Usher family home, and of Roderick and Madeline. For example, the house is called a "mansion of gloom"; Roderick is described as having "a ghastly pallor of the skin" and hair of "wild gossamer texture"; and Madeline, who the narrator sees only briefly before she dies, stirs up feelings of dread. Although the narrator is unsettled, shocked, and taken aback by his surroundings from the very beginning of the story, it is not clear what is causing such trepidation. When Roderick attempts to explain the cause of his "nervous agitation," he states that it is "a constitutional and family evil," suggesting that he and Madeline are somehow cursed. Some have speculated that the evil behind this "curse" is a long history of incest or family inbreeding within the Usher line and that both Roderick and Madeline are suffering the physical and emotional consequences of behavior almost universally condemned as immoral. Others, however, have stated that the evil permeating the story is of purely supernatural origin and that Roderick's hysteria is not imagined but is a justifiable reaction to otherworldly forces.

The atmosphere of terror in the story is heightened by the ambiguity of Madeline's character— she can be viewed with sympathy, because of her illness, or with suspicion. Some critics have even suggested that she is a vampire attempting to sap the life force from Roderick. The narrator also heightens the aura of evil in "The Fall of the House of Usher" because while he tries to view the situation objectively and rationally, despite his increasing feelings of foreboding, he ultimately succumbs to the evil pervading the Usher home. Some critics have, in fact, stated that the narrator himself is evil and that he, along with Roderick, knowingly buried Madeline alive and that he is deliberately trying to deceive the reader about what happened.

Madness and Insanity

The themes of madness and insanity grow from Poe's depiction of Roderick's increasingly unstable mental and emotional breakdown. Roderick is afflicted with numerous mysterious maladies. He suffers, as the narrator states, from "a morbid acuteness of the senses," and he is overwhelmed by feelings of fear and anxiety. Roderick's agitated mental state is also due, in part, to Madeline's fatal illness, which causes her to become cataleptic—a state of extreme muscle rigidity and apparent unconsciousness. As the story progresses, Roderick attempts to relate his fear to the narrator and engages in numerous activities—including playing the guitar, creating a disturbing painting, and composing a lyric entitled "The Haunted Palace"—in an attempt to calm himself. He also reads books on the supernatural and the occult. As Roderick becomes increasingly hysterical, both the narrator and the reader are left to speculate on the causes of such strange behavior. It remains unclear, however, if Roderick's malady is a psychological reaction to an incestual relationship with his sister or if he is, indeed, being possessed by evil forces. Nevertheless, Poe's portrayal of Roderick's deterioration raises important questions about the causes, stages, and effects of insanity.

Style

"The Fall of the House of Usher" centers on Roderick Usher and his twin sister Madeline, the last surviving members of the Usher family.

Setting

The setting of "The Fall of the House of Usher" plays an integral part in the story because it establishes an atmosphere of dreariness, melancholy, and decay. The story takes place in the Usher family mansion, which is isolated and located in a "singularly dreary tract of country." The house immediately stirs up in the narrator "a sense of insufferable gloom," and it is described as having "bleak walls," "vacant eye-like windows," and "minute *fungi* overspread [on] the whole exterior." The interior of the house is equally dreary, with "vaulted and fretted" ceilings, "dark draperies hung upon the walls," and furniture that is "comfortless, antique, and tattered." Roderick is also disturbed by the setting, believing that the house is one of the causes of his nervous agitation. The narrator notes that Roderick "was enchained by certain superstitious impressions in regard to the dwelling which he tenanted, and whence, for many years, he had never ventured forth."

Point of View

"The Fall of the House of Usher" is told from the point of view of the unnamed narrator, who, being skeptical and rational, doesn't want to believe that there are supernatural causes to what is happening around him. Although he tries to tell the reader that Roderick's anxiety and nervousness are simply symptoms of the latter's mental anguish, the narrator, and therefore the reader, becomes increasingly disturbed as the story progresses. By telling the story from the point of view of a skeptic rather than a believer, Poe increases the suspense as well as the emotional impact of the story's ending.

Media Adaptations

- "The Fall of the House of Usher" was adapted to film in 1952. Directed and produced by Ivan Barnett, this black and white, 70-minute film starred Kay Tendeter as Roderick Usher and Gwen Watford as Madeline Usher and is available from Vigilant distributors. It is generally considered to be apoor adaptation of Poe's story.

- Considered one of the best film adaptations of "The Fall of the House of Usher," the 1960 version starred Vincent Price, Myrna Fahey, and Mark Damon and was directed by Mark Corman. It runs 65 minutes and is in color.

- The story was also adapted to film in 1980. Starring Martin Landau as Roderick Usher and Dimitra Arliss as Madeline Usher, this 101-minute color film was produced by Charles E. Sellier, Jr. and directed by James L. Conway. It is available from Sunn Classic.

- A dramatization of "The Fall of the House of Usher" was taped in 1965 as part of the "American Story Classics" series. Available from Film Video Library, this adaptation runs 29 minutes and is in black and white.

- Another dramatization of the story was taped in 1976 by Encyclopaedia Britannica Educational Corporation. Also produced by Britannica in 1976, *The Fall of the House of Usher: A Discussion* features science fiction writer Ray Bradbury discussing the Gothic traditions of "The Fall of the House of Usher" as well as Poe's influence on contemporary science fiction.

Symbolism

Poe uses symbolism—a literary technique where an object, person, or concept represents something else—throughout "The Fall of the House of Usher." The Usher mansion is the most important symbol in the story; isolated, decayed and full of the atmosphere of death, the house represents the dying Usher family itself. The narrator emphasizes this when he notes that "about the whole mansion and domain there hung an atmosphere peculiar to themselves and their immediate vicinity—an atmosphere which had no affinity with the air of heaven, but which had reeked up from the decayed trees, and the grey wall, and the silent tarn." The fissure in the house is also an important symbol. Although it is, at first, barely visible to the narrator, it suggests a fundamental split or fault in the twin personalities of the last surviving Ushers and foretells the final ruin of the house and family. Other notable symbols of death and madness are Roderick's lyric, "The Haunted Palace"; his abstract painting, which is described as a "phantasmagoric" conception by the narrator; and the "fantastic character" of his guitar playing.

Imagery

Poe uses imagery to create a foreboding atmosphere and to advance his themes in the story. An image is a concrete representation of an object or sensory experience; images help evoke the feelings associated with the object or the experience itself. For example, when the narrator briefly sees Madeline, he states: "The lady Madeline passed slowly through the remote portion of the apartment, and, without having noticed my presence, disappeared. . . . A sensation of stupor oppressed me, and my eyes followed her retreating steps." Such images contribute to the perception that Madeline is ghostlike and mysterious. When the narrator sees the physician on the stair at the beginning of the story, he notes: "His countenance, I thought, wore a mingled expression of low cunning and perplexity. He accosted me with trepidation and passed on." This image of the doctor is much more effective than a mere literal description; it underscores the fear and anxiety pervading the Usher home.

Gothicism

"The Fall of the House of Usher" is considered a preeminent example of Gothic short fiction with its focus on such topics as incest, terminal illness, mental breakdown, and death. Gothic fiction generally includes elements of horror, the supernatural, gloom, and violence and creates in the reader feelings of terror and dread. Gothic fiction also frequently takes place in medieval-like settings; the desolate, ancient, and decaying Usher mansion is ideally suited for this story. In addition to creating an atmosphere of dread, Poe, some critics have suggested, incorporated into his story aspects of the vampire tale. J. O. Bailey, for example, contended in *American Literature* that Madeline is a vampire and that Roderick is fighting her powers "with all he has."

Historical Context

"The Fall of the House of Usher" was first published in 1839 in *Burton's Gentleman's Magazine*. At a time when most popular literature was highly moralistic, Poe's stories were concerned only with creating emotional effects. Poe charged that most of his contemporaries were "didactic," that is, they were preoccupied with making religious or political statements in their writings to the detriment of the fiction itself. His own tales of terror, in which he often depicted the psychological disintegration of unstable or emotionally overwrought characters, were in sharp contrast to the works of more highly praised writers of the time. Because of Poe's disdain for didactic writing, he was little regarded by the literary establishment in his day.

But despite being dismissed by literary critics, Poe's tales were instrumental in establishing the short story as a viable literary form. Before his time, such short works were not regarded as serious literature. Poe's examples of what the short story could accomplish, and his own nonfiction writings about the form, were instrumental in establishing the short story as a legitimate form of serious literature. Poe had a strong influence in popular fiction as well. His tales of terror are considered among the finest ever produced in the horror genre. He also pioneered, some critics say invented, the genre of detective fiction with his story "The

Murders in the Rue Morgue."

During the time Poe was writing, a distinct and mature body of American literature was beginning to develop with the contributions of such authors as Poe, Nathaniel Hawthorne, John Greenleaf Whittier, Harriet Beecher Stowe, Henry Wadsworth Longfellow, and James Fenimore Cooper. Before this time, American readers considered British literature the only serious literature available. American writers wrote imitations derived from British models. But with the advent of a new group of American writers who were writing about specifically American subjects, settings, and characters, a distinctly American literature began to emerge. Poe was one of the American writers of the time who helped to formulate this national literature.

Topics for Further Study

- Examine the lyric "The Haunted

Palace" written by Roderick Usher in "The Fall of the House of Usher" and discuss how it reflects Roderick's mental and emotional state.

- Read the short story "The Yellow Wallpaper" (1892) by Charlotte Perkins Gilman and compare and contrast the portrayal of mental breakdown in each story.
- Poe's fictional works and critical theories greatly impacted nineteenth-century literature, particularly the French symbolist movement. Research and discuss Poe's influence on such French writers as Charles Baudelaire and Paul Valery.

Critical Overview

While Poe's works were not widely acclaimed during his lifetime, he did earn respect as a gifted fiction writer and poet, especially after the publication of his poem "The Raven." After his death, however, the history of his critical reception becomes one of dramatically uneven judgements and interpretations. This was, in part, the fault of Poe's one-time friend and literary executor R. W. Griswold, who, in an obituary notice bearing the byline "Lud-wig," attributed the depravity and psychological peculiarities of many of the characters in Poe's fiction to Poe himself. In retrospect, Griswold's insults seem to have elicited as much sympathy as censure, leading subsequent biographers of the late nineteenth century to defend, sometimes avidly, Poe's name.

It was not until the 1941 biography by A. H. Quinn, *Edgar Allan Poe: A Critical Autobiography,* that a balanced view was provided of Poe, his work, and the relationship between the author's life and his imagination. Nevertheless, the identification of Poe with the murderers and madmen of his works survived and flourished in the twentieth century, most notably in the form of psychoanalytical studies by such critics as Marie Bonaparte and Joseph Wood Krutch. Added to the controversy over Poe's sanity was the question of the value of Poe's works as serious literature. Among Poe's detractors were such eminent literary figures as Henry James,

Aldous Huxley, and T. S. Eliot, who dismissed Poe's works as juvenile, vulgar, and artistically debased; in contrast, these same works were judged to be of the highest literary merit by such writers as George Bernard Shaw and William Carlos Williams. Complementing Poe's erratic reputation among American and English critics was the generally more elevated opinion of critics elsewhere in the world, particularly in France. Following the extensive translations and commentaries of French poet Charles Baudelaire in the 1850s, Poe's works were received with high esteem by French writers, especially those associated with the late nineteenth-century symbolist movement, who admired Poe's transcendent aspirations as a poet. In other countries, Poe enjoyed similar regard, and numerous studies have been written tracing the influence of the American author on international literature.

Today, Poe is regarded as one of the foremost progenitors of modern literature, both in its popular forms, such as horror and detective fiction, and in its more complex and self-conscious forms, such as poetry and criticism. In contrast to earlier critics who viewed the man and his works as one, recent criticism has developed a view of Poe as a detached artist who was more concerned with displaying his writing talents than with expressing his feelings. While at one time critics wished to remove Poe from literary history, his works remain integral to any conception of modernism in world literature.

Compare & Contrast

- **1830s:** Common belief dictates that odors from water—such as the tarn outside the Usher house—could cause mental illness of the type suffered by Roderick Usher. Few, if any, effective treatments were available for mental illness.

  Today: Better understanding of the physiological causes of mental illness and a variety of medical therapies result in a vast improvement in the way the mentally ill are treated.

- **1830s:** The deceased are commonly laid in-state at home for several days. Funeral homes are rare; families prepare and bury their loved ones themselves.

  Today: Most people the in hospitals and wakes are most often held in churches or funeral homes.

- **1830s:** Travel is difficult, slow, and sometimes dangerous. Railroads are in their infancy and most long distance travel is in horse-drawn wagons. It was not unusual for guests to stay several weeks or for an entire season when invited to a relative's or friend's house.

Today: Improved transportation—including railroads, airplanes, and automobiles—makes longdistance travel easier, while advanced communications technology like telephones and e-mail makes long visits with family and friends less popular than in previous eras.

What Do I Read Next?

- Poe's epic poem "The Raven," published in 1845, centers on a young scholar who is emotionally tormented by a raven's ominous repetition of the word "nevermore" in answer to his question about the probability of an afterlife with his deceased lover.

- Poe's "Ligeia" is a long poem in which a husband narrates the story of his beautiful dead wife who returns from the grave and assumes the identity of his second wife.

- "Young Goodman Brown" is a story by Nathaniel Hawthorne, a contemporary of Poe. Written in 1835, it concerns a newly married Puritan in New England who ventures forth one night against the wishes of his wife, Faith, and encounters several of his neighbors conducting satanic rituals in the woods.

- Stephen King's novel *The Shining* (1977) tells how the evil forces in a remote resort hotel manipulate the alcoholic caretaker into attempting to murder his wife and child.

- The short story "The Shunned House" by H. P. Lovecraft centers on a house possessed by evil powers. The somewhat Gothic horror story was inspired by "The Fall of the House of Usher" and Nathaniel Hawthorne's *House of the Seven Gables,* in which a haunted house inflicts terror upon its inhabitants.

Further Reading

Abel, Darrel. "A Key to the House of Usher," in *University of Toronto Quarterly*, Vol. XVII, No. 2, January, 1949, pp. 176-85.

> Abel talks about the setting of "'The Fall of the House of Usher," and how the themes of isolation and self-destructive concentration are symbolized by the character of Roderick Usher.

Baym, Nina. "The Fall of the House of Usher,' Character Analysis," in *The Norton Anthology of American Literature,* W. W. Norton, 1995, p. 664.

> Baym offers a brief analysis of the three characters and their mental disorders.

Bieganowski, Ronald. "The Self-consuming Narrator in Poe's 'Ligeia' and Usher'," *in American Literature,* Volume 60, No. 2, May, 1988, pp. 175-87.

> Bieganowski shows how the narrators in these two tales become enamored of their own rhetoric and therefore fail to tell the tale in the complete manner they intend. They fail because their desire to tell their story in the most ideal manner possible overwhelms the story itself.

Brennan, Matthew C. "Turnerian Topography: The Paintings of Roderick Usher," in *Studies in Short Fiction,* Volume 27, Fall, 1990, pp. 605-8.

> Brennan argues that Poe's descriptions of Roderick's paintings show a strong similarity to the paintings of Englishman Joseph Turner. He believes that both Poe and Turner reject the realist's approach to their art in favor of a more vague, expressionist approach called the "sublime style."

Brooks, Cleanth, Jr. and Robert Penn Warren. "The Fall of the House of Usher," in their *Understanding Fiction,* New York, F.S. Crofts & Co., 1943, pp. 202-5.

> Reduces "'The Fall of the House of Usher" to a "relatively meaningless" horror story which serves principally as a case study in morbid psychology and lacks any quality of pathos or tragedy.

Evans, Walter. "The Fall of the House of Usher' and Poe's Theory of the Tale, "in *Studies in Short Fiction,* Volume 14, No. 2, Spring, 1977, pp. 137-44.

> Evans contends that there are significant discrepancies between Poe's theory of the tale and his literary practice as exemplified by "The Fall of the House of Usher."

May, Leila S. "Sympathies of Scarcely Intelligible Nature: The Brother-Sister Bond in Poe's "'Fall of the House of Usher'," in *Studies in Short Fiction,* Volume 30, Summer, 1993, pp. 387-96.

> May makes the relationship of the Ushers and their fall a symbolic representation of the fall of the family in the 19th century.

Poe, Edgar Allan. "The Philosophy of Composition" in *Selected Writings of Edgar Allan Poe,* edited by Edward H. Davidson, Houghton, 1956, pp. 452-61.

> Poe outlines his philosophy of literary composition, discussing the proper length and content of literary works.

Rout, Kay Kinsella. "The Unreliable and Unbalanced Narrator," in *Studies in Short Fiction,* Volume 19, Winter, 1982, pp. 27-33.

> While this article is more about John Gardner's story, "The Ravages of Spring," Rout compares the narrator in it to the narrator of "Usher." She sees both as unreliable and emotionally unbalanced.

Voloshin, Beverly R. "Explanation in 'The Fall of the House of Usher'," in *Studies in Short Fiction,* Volume 23, Fall, 1986, pp. 419-28.

> Voloshin argues that the story is a turning point in the development of

the Gothic tale in the hands of Poe. She says it contains all the necessary ingredients: romance, mystery, darkness, supernatural, decay, a corpse, and even vampirism.

Lightning Source UK Ltd.
Milton Keynes UK
UKHW020859210719
346492UK00006B/50/P